L.I.D MAGAZINE

LUXURIOUS INTERIOR DESIGNS

NOVEMBER 2020

TOP 5
FAVES

CLEANING
TIPS

HOLIDAY
TIPS

WELCOME TO

LUXURIOUS INTERIOR DESIGNS MAGAZINE ALSO KNOWN AS L.I.D MAGAZINE,

Sherron Bernard

Introduction

Hi, I'm Sherron Bernard, the proud owner of Luxurious interior designs located in the Inland Empire. I've been serving our community for over 5 years helping dreams come true without breaking the bank. This is my passion. While there is plenty of money to be made in this industry, it's not my first chose. My joy comes from the happiness of my clients in any way that I can help. What I love most about my job is I get the chance to build long-lasting relationships with my clients, where we all then become more like family. I can't explain to you the joy I feel when each project is complete and my clients are overwhelmed with joy to see their vision come to life at a fraction of the cost that they originally anticipated. That is the best feeling in the world to me! That is also what has inspired me to create this magazine; to help motivate you to make your dreams a reality and by inspiring and motivating you to achieve the goals you have set for you and your home. I believe in you and I want to help you too. In each article, you will find tips and tricks to help you achieve your vision. If you have any questions or would like to see how to do a project, please email me at Luxurious_interior_designs_@yahoo.com and I will do my best to help. Thank you and I hope you enjoy.

TABLE OF CONTENT

CHEERS TO
THE SEASON

As the warm summer months fade away and Fall brings the cool breeze along with our beautiful falling leaves, pumpkins are just about ready to be carved out and set at the dinner table. Over the years, the traditional orange and brown Thanksgiving celebration is now a thing of the past. You are now free to express yourself freely with the colors of your choice. My hope is to help you out by delving into your creativity to create your own space that you can enjoy with your friends and family. Here are a few tips to decorating yours space for the season.

TIP 1 ________________

Choose your color theme :

When it comes to choosing your colors, it's OK to choose what is trending or you can think outside the box and create the new up and coming trend. Don't be afraid of what others may think of your style. Not everyone will like your style, and that is OK. But some will like it and the few who do may be inspired to be creative. You just might be the next one to start the new trend! Choose your colors by what has recently caught your eye most often and pay attention to how the colors makes you feel. You would be surprised at how much color effects our moods. Try to choose neutral colors when it comes to your bigger and bolder pieces. Choose your smaller inexpensive items in the color of your chose for the season. The reason I give this tip is because 9 times out of 10, you won't be using the same colors next season or the next year, this can reduce the clutter.

TIP 2 ________________

Choose your Décor :

When it comes to choosing home décor, especially seasonal décor, I like to tell my clients "take your time purchasing your décor pieces." Also, get what you want; don't just buy something trying to compensate for what you really want. The only thing that will happen when you settle for items that you really didn't want in the first place, is you will end up spending more money continuing to buy more that you don't want or need at the time, creating clutter, only to then end up getting what you really wanted in the first place. But now the other items don't have a space in your home leaving you with a mess and a house full of clutter. So, we can cut out the extra pieces and save some money by taking your time and researching your items before making a purchase. Also, do price comparisons to get the best deal with the best quality.

TIP 3 ________________

Choose your space :

When it comes to choosing your spaces to decorate for the season there are usually multiple spaces to decorate. Purchase items with a space in mind. The most common spaces are the front porch, back patio, kitchen and bathrooms with a few pieces in the living room, and/or family/ entertainment room. That can become quite expensive each season, year after year, even shopping at Dollar Tree. I believe most of us would love to do this every season, and some do, but how do we do this without breaking the bank? If you purchase items that you can use all year long then as the seasons change you can simply "shop" your existing décor in your home, and maybe use a can of spray paint to update the color or add some fabrics as accent. You can save a ton of money and still achieve the beautiful look you desire. Do price comparisons and budget accordingly before the upcoming season. Remember quality over quantity is key. Choose pieces that you can use all year long in various places throughout your home.

This Months DIY project was partnered with a great company, **Delta Water Restoration Service.** I want to give a special thank you to Jason, Scott, Tim and Matt for coming to the rescue and helping me put together my vision after we discovered that my kitchen cabinets had sustained water damage. The kitchen turned out beautiful. This month's DIY is a kitchen update. The kitchen before had served its purpose for about 3 years. It was still functional; however, it needed a little TLC. The vision for this room was to update the paint from light grey to white for a more clean and brighter look. My style preference at this time is a combination of luxury, modern, and traditional, so I wanted to change out the diamond hardware to a more modern brushed satin nickel finished hardware. And last but not,

less paint and lower the center island to a counter height. Now that sounds simple right? However, even as a designer you just never know what's going to happen in the middle of these projects. But don't let that stop you from achieving your vision. Just be sure that when planning your budget for projects to put in a contingency category for unexpected expenses and put a fair amount there; at least half of the coast of the project for two reasons: 1) You probably won't need that much extra to fix any unknown problems and 2) Best case, if you don't have to use it all, then when your project is done you will have more money to add to the next projects unknown expense category and it just keeps going. It really helps us in completing our projects.

Before Pictures

The project started out smoothly, we were able to paint the upper and lower cabinets against the wall and install the hardware with no issues in just 2 days. I knew it would only take me another day, maybe two, with the island after we cut it down to counter height. The rest should be easy since it would only take me about 20 minutes to paint, let it dry overnight, and install the hardware 24 hours later. But it didn't quite work out that way. As I went to paint the island, I noticed that the cabinets were quite wet. I know we had a problem with the dishwasher, so we had already purchased a new one, as well as upgraded all other the appliances, before starting the project. However, we had no idea that it was so wet. We then decided to call **Delta Water Restoration Service** to the rescue.

Even though, I'm a California-licensed Interior Designer, and it's something I could have easily done myself, it's best to know when it's time to call in the professionals for specific jobs and this was one of them. Long story short, we had a bad water leak coming from the dishwasher line and it damaged all the island cabinets. The cabinets needed to be replaced before a bigger issue occurred. However, despite the unexpected, the project turned out amazing. I designed the counter cuts for the new island, which is what we had planned to do in the beginning when we were going to cut it down to counter height. But, **Delta Water Restoration Service** did everything for us. I feel we did save time and energy on other projects. If you want to see the other projects that we worked on please check out December's upcoming issue where you can find out more tips, tricks and DIY projects.

Doing what you love is freedom, loving what you do is happiness.

> Do something today
> that your future self
> will thank you for.

This month's photo is from my personal master bedroom. My style at this present time is luxury, traditional mixed with a little modern. You can have a high-end look without breaking the bank. I just love staying in luxury hotels, but they can be expensive. I thought why not bring the luxury home. I feel that I have achieved that. The colors may change a little here and there, but for the most part, the bigger items are a neutral luxury color as well as universal. They can be used in various places throughout my home to give a new look and feel. I love to shop my home.

The lamps I have had for a few years. They were a brown color, but I simply got a can of metallic

silver spray paint from my local homeware store and after two coats of paint and two new lamp shades I can now get more years of life out of these pieces.

With mirrors, life is endless. Once I'm ready to move on to new design, I can use these anywhere in my home. The wonderful thing about the mirrors is that I can also change the direction to give a different look and feel.

The pillows can be used again elsewhere on a chair, indoors or outdoors, or in an office. If I don't like the color when I'm done with this current design, I can simply change the fabric for a new look. There are endless possibilities.

When it comes to bedding, I love to layer my beds for many reasons. But just to name a few:

1. Conformability: Layering thinner blankets allow you to customize what is most comfortable for the best night's sleep. I don't have to use all the blankets that are on the bed at the time. If it's a colder night, I can use all of the blankets. If it's a warmer night, I can just use the top blanket.

2. Color theme: I'm able to get the colors that I want at the time without having to change all the bedding.

3. Luxury : I get the luxury look of a hotel room.

4. Motivation: It motivates me to want to make my bed every morning.

5. Inspiration: When I make my bed in the morning, every time I walk past my bedroom it always inspires me to want to maintain the rest of my home. It's a great feeling.

I hope you enjoyed this month's photo of the month. If you would like to see one of your photo in L.I.D's photo of the month category, please email me your photos at luxurious_ interior_designs@yahoo.com. You just might be featured in next month's magazine! It is limited to one photo per month. Upon submission, please tell me about your space and what it does for you.

MY FAVORITE OF
THE MONTH

This month's favorites for me are in the cleaning department. There are many great brands out there that I have tried and we will revisit them soon. However, at this moment, I am really loving the **Method** cleaner system. One of the reasons that I like it is because if I need more, I can easily run to my local Target and pick up another cleaner. They offer a variety of cleaners in just about every area of cleaning that needs to be done from wood floors to countertops and everything in between. Their products smell amazing too! You can also order online where they can send it directly to your home (automatic reorder is available as well). These products don't use any harsh chemicals, leaving your home smelling clean and fresh all day without harming your health or the environment. What more could you ask for! This is definitely one of my favorites. If you haven't tried them out, I recommend you do. **Highly Recommend (Not Sponsored)**

BEST FINDS

1

Leopard Modern Pu Leather adjustable swivel bar stools

This is an Amazon find. You get a set of 2 for $84.99. I purchased 2 sets of 2. They are really great quality and come in two colors at the moment: white and light grey. I purchased the light grey, and to me, they were the best find of the 5 listed. They are very easy to assemble...almost too easy!
Highly Recommended

3D Damsk Wallpaper Modern

Coming in at number 2 is also an Amazon find. This 3D wallpaper is so beautiful and can be used in various places in the home. I chose to use this gorgeous wallpaper in both my updated kitchen and entry hallway. As you can see, it stands alone beautifully, but with the right décor pieces, the wall can still stand out and compliment any wall art as well. The only downfall to this wallpaper is that you must buy the adhesive separately. It was still at great find in my opinion because you get a lot of wall coverage and the price was great at $29.99. **Highly Recommended**

Home Goods Decorative plates

Coming in at number 3 are these two amazingly beautiful decorative plates that I found at Home Goods. These plates were found at the great price of $12.99 each. As you can see, you can also use these plates in various locations in your home. They can be used for many years due to the more neutral colors. **Highly Recommended**

Better Home Essential Oil Diffuser

Coming in at number 4 Is the Better Home Essential Oil Diffuser. It is a great price ($20) for the luxury look that I was going for. Now Better Home's has a variety of home products, including a variety of diffusers, with prices ranging from around $6.00 up to $45.00, depending on the style. I did my research for about a month before making my purchase. I wanted a diffuser, but not just any diffuser. I wanted one that would complement my home as well as serve its purpose of making the home smell fresh for hours at a time. This particular one is a plugin, so I don't have to keep purchasing batteries. It also lights up in about seven different colors with the option to change colors automatically at the click of a button. I just love how I can change the mood with one click. This diffuser will run for about two hours at a time and keep the house smelling good for about 3 to 4 hours without having to refill. Better Home products can be found at a variety of shopping centers. I picked mine up at my local Wal-Mart. **Highly Recommended**

5

Christian Siriano New York Reversible Fur Blanket

Last but not least, coming in at number 5 are these two beautiful Christian Siriano Reversible Blankets. Might I say, they feel amazing. They offer a relaxing comfort when sleeping. They also offer two colors for a change in style. I purchased two different styles; one offering me this beautiful darker grey and white and the other being a white and tan on the other side giving me a chance to change things up as the seasons change. I purchased two king size comforters at an amazing price of $29.99 each from a local mom and pop discount store. The reason I'm listing these items from a local mom and pop store is for us to keep in mind to check out the local stores. You just never know what you might find! Some of these stores have high end ticket items at discounted prices that you wouldn't believe and they're by the same companies just a lower price. Why pay more when you can pay less. **Highly Recommended**

TIPS IN
CLEANING

We all have our day to day cleaning routine and our seasonal cleaning routine. I would like to share some tips that can hopefully make your cleaning routine a little easier than usual. This helps me on a day to day basis. If you have some tips that you would like to share, please do so by emailing me at Luxuirous_interior_designs@yahoo.com. I would love to hear from you and possibly share your tips in one of our upcoming magazines.

TIP 1

Start at least one load of laundry every morning. It will keep the laundry at an all-time low and you won't feel so overwhelmed with doing the laundry. It will no longer look like a chore, now it becomes a routine.

TIP 2

Do the dishes the night before. You may not be in the mood to do them, but trust me, your tomorrow self will thank you because you really won't want to do them in the morning either. Plus, you will sleep better and wake up more refreshed knowing it is done. How do I know you will sleep better? Because when you go to bed with things on your mind you toss and turn more often than if you went to sleep with some relaxing jazz music playing in the background and knowing chores are done. Think about what you are thinking about the next time before you go to bed. These are facts.

TIP 3

Check your cabinets once a week and toss any empty containers, bottles and loose trash out. To be honest, I check daily as I enter a cabinet because it's just easier for me to do it as I see it so that it doesn't build up on me. It's one less chore I have to plan to clean.

TIP 4

If you feel like your home is a complete disaster at this moment and you are asking yourself how do I just start or get motivated when you don't want to do it, then here are a few tips:

- There are thousands of "Clean with Me" videos on YouTube, myself being one of them. You can find a few under my top 5 YouTubers of the month category of this magazine. I encourage you to find one who motivates you to clean with them. The "Clean with Me" videos can be a very helpful tool to help you get your home back in order. You can learn a lot of tips and tricks to getting and keeping your home the way you like it.

- Be honest with yourself about each item in your home. Do you really need each item you are picking up? What service is it serving you in your home? Keep in mind the more you keep the more you have to maintain. Because everything should have a place in your home and should serve a purpose in your home and life, if it doesn't serve a purpose any longer, then it's time to go.

- Pay attention to the different items in your home that friends and family say they like. So, when the item has served its purpose in your home and it's time to move on you can bless those people with the item they loved so much. Or you can donate the items to any local donation centers in your hometown. I'm sure a needy family would love to have them.

TIP 5

Get rid of items while they're in good condition. It will be easier to sell or donate to someone else when the items are in good condition. Do a yard sale. But take a few dollars to pick up a few cans of neutral spray paint (white, grey, tan, brown) and do some touch ups on your old items to make them look like new again. The items will sell faster, I promise you. However, don't jack up the price by 10 or 20 dollars because of a few cents of spray paint. You might pay $2.00 to $6.00 for the paint but you will get a lot of items covered for that price. Be reasonable with your pricing and keep the goal in mind. What's the goal?? To declutter and get your home back in order.

- If you enjoyed these tips please check out next month's tips in cleaning category for more helpful tips and tricks to getting and keeping your home in order.

CREATE YOUR SPACE TO FIT YOUR NEEDS, EXPRESS YOURSELF IN A WAY THAT IS FUNCTIONABLE FOR YOU AND YOUR FAMILY.

Don't limit yourself on your designs. What you see in your mind, you can bring to life and it doesn't have to cost a arm and a leg. Do take your time with your décor. Shop responsibly and budget for your items. Remember this is not a sprint but this is a marathon, there is no rush to perfect your space. I can assure you that you wont be put out of your home, if your home is not decorated by a certain time. So take your time and have fun. I am here to help.

RECOMMEND IN THE HIGH DESERT AND INLAND EMPIRE, CALIFORNIA
SERVING INLAND EMPIRE
SERVING HIGH DESERT

happy
holidays